THE MAGERMAN EDITION

תנ״ך קורן הסיפור המצויר
THE KOREN TANAKH GRAPHIC NOVEL

YONA • יונה

DAVID SACKS
Writer

LARISA KERZHNER • AVI BLYER
DAVE YOUKOVICH • AARON MINIER
Artists

YAEL NATHAN • SHANI GRIM
Colorists

ROB LEIGH
Letterer

TZIPORA GINZBERG
Managing Editor

JORDAN B. GORFINKEL
Creator & Editor

JEWISH CARTOON .com

ירושלים KOREN

Yona Graphic Novel
First Hebrew/English Edition © 2024

Koren Publishers Jerusalem Ltd.
POB 4044, Jerusalem 91040, ISRAEL
POB 8531, New Milford, CT 06776, USA

www.korenpub.com

The creation of this book was made possible with the generous support of The Jewish Book Trust.

Hardcover, ISBN 978 965 7767 83 2

Printed in TURKEY
YGN01

May this unique and creative presentation of
the Yona story serve as an inspiration
to dive into the many layers and depths present within the story
and glean valuable messages from each of its verses.
May the portrayal of the story allow the reader
to connect with the Creator in prayer and gratitude,
as Yona states:

"But I, voicing thanks, shall bring You offerings."
(Yona 2:10)

David, Debra, Elijah, Zachary, Sydney, and Lexie Magerman

PROLOGUES

AND GOD CREATED THE GREAT SEA CREATURES...
...AND ALL THE KINDS OF CRAWLING, LIVING THINGS THAT SWARM IN THE WATER.
AND GOD SAW THAT THIS WAS GOOD.
THERE WAS EVENING, AND THERE WAS MORNING~ THE FIFTH DAY.
Bereshit 1:21,23; see Pirkei DeRabbi Eliezer 10

וַיִּבְרָ֣א אֱלֹהִ֔ים בראשית א:כא
אֶת־הַתַּנִּינִ֖ם הַגְּדֹלִ֑ים
וְאֵ֣ת כָּל־נֶ֣פֶשׁ הַֽחַיָּ֣ה ׀ הָֽרֹמֶ֡שֶׂת
אֲשֶׁר֩ שָֽׁרְצ֨וּ הַמַּ֜יִם לְמִֽינֵהֶ֗ם...
וַיַּ֥רְא אֱלֹהִ֖ים כִּי־טֽוֹב׃

וַֽיְהִי־עֶ֥רֶב וַֽיְהִי־בֹ֖קֶר י֥וֹם חֲמִישִֽׁי׃ בראשית א:כג

* עיין בפרקי דרבי אליעזר י

IN THE DAYS AFTER
KING SOLOMON BUILT
THE HOLY TEMPLE...

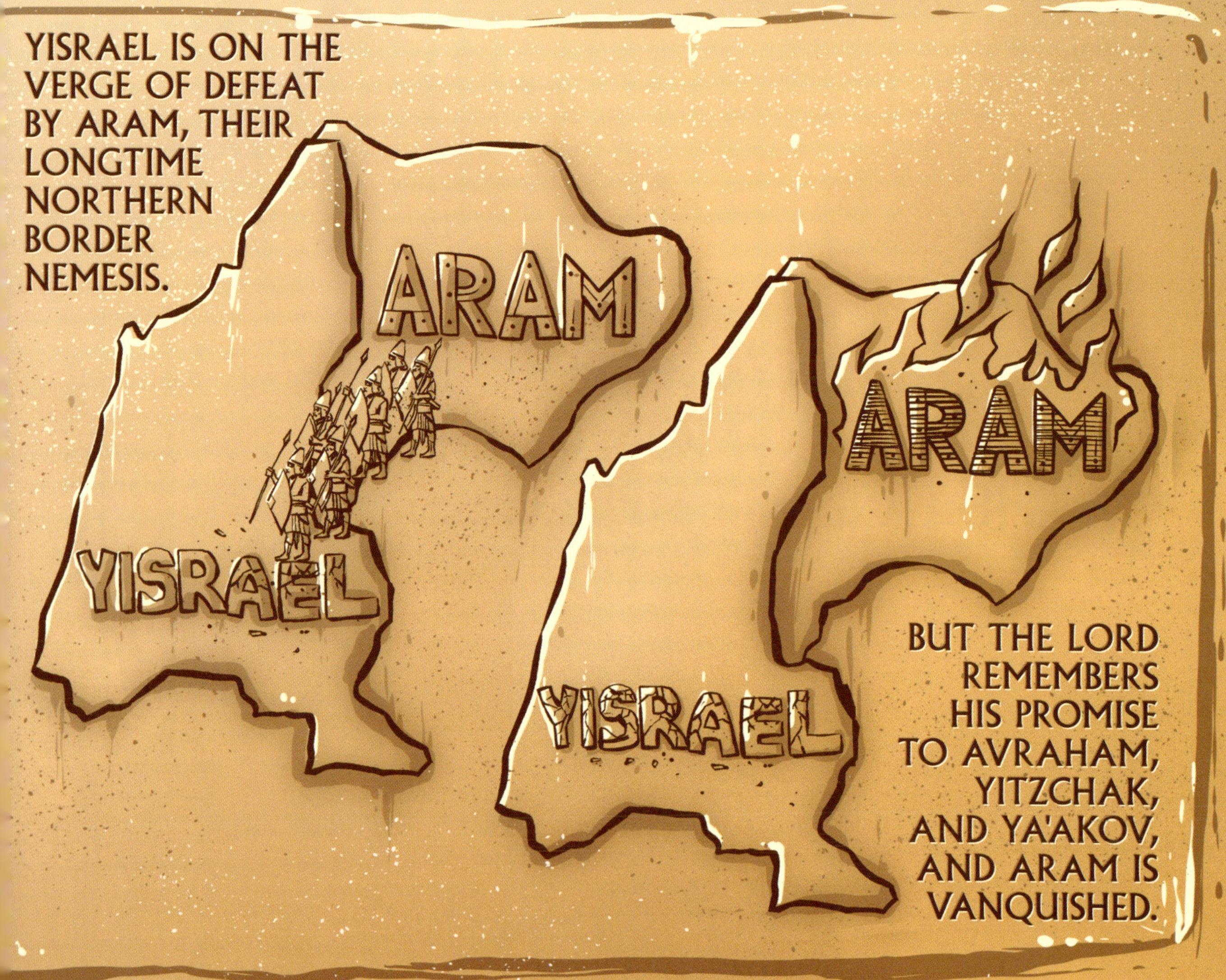
YISRAEL IS ON THE VERGE OF DEFEAT BY ARAM, THEIR LONGTIME NORTHERN BORDER NEMESIS.
ARAM
YISRAEL
ARAM
YISRAEL
BUT THE LORD REMEMBERS HIS PROMISE TO AVRAHAM, YITZCHAK, AND YA'AKOV, AND ARAM IS VANQUISHED.

YET THE JEWISH PEOPLE STILL SIN.
THE ASSYRIANS, TOO, ARE EVIL IN THE EYES OF THE LORD.

...THE JEWISH NATION SPLITS INTO TWO KINGDOMS: YISRAEL AND YEHUDA.
YISRAEL SINS GREATLY.

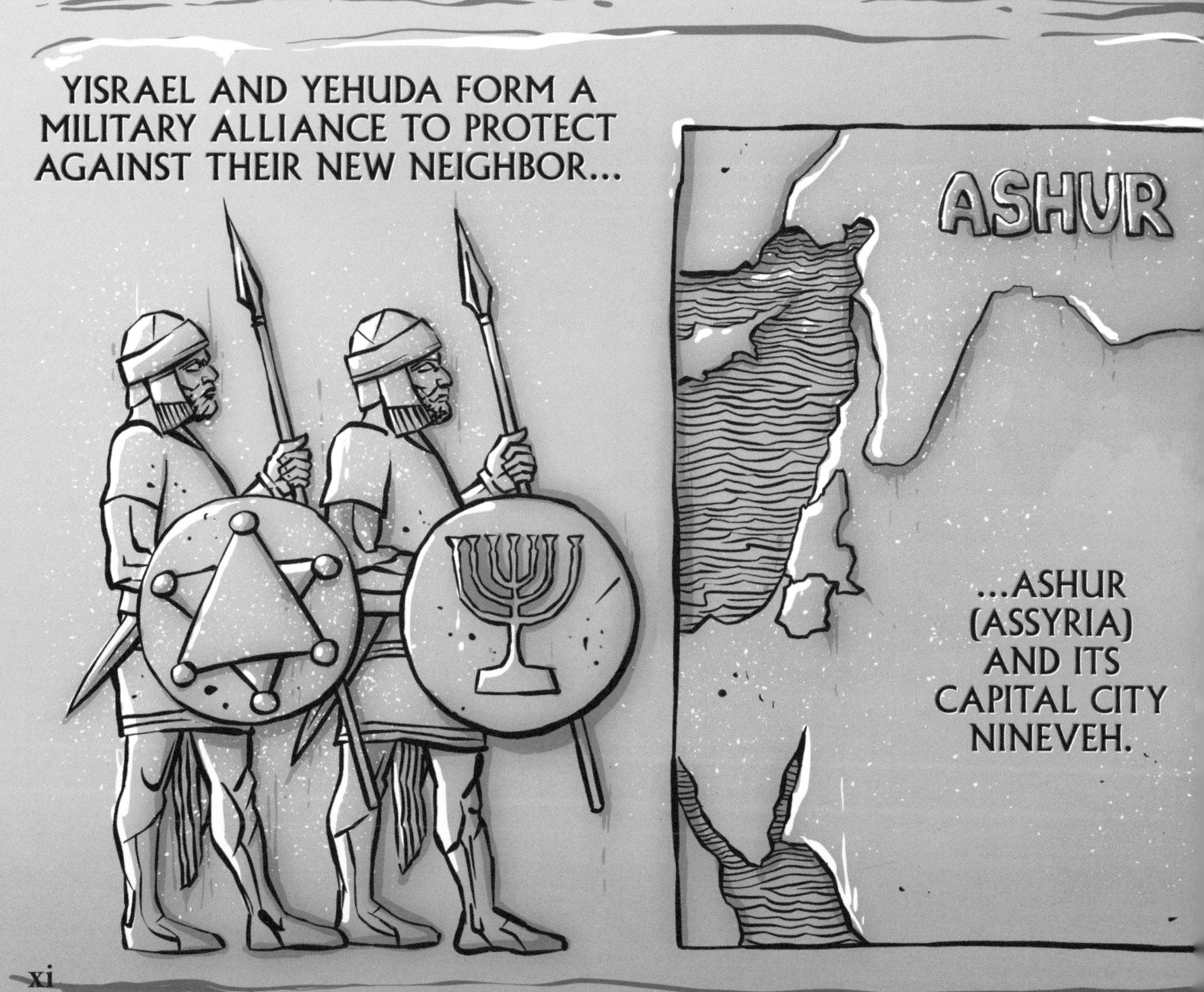
YISRAEL AND YEHUDA FORM A MILITARY ALLIANCE TO PROTECT AGAINST THEIR NEW NEIGHBOR...
ASHUR
...ASHUR (ASSYRIA) AND ITS CAPITAL CITY NINEVEH.

WHICHEVER NATION REPENTS SHALL VANQUISH THE OTHER, AND BECOME THE NEXT GREAT WORLD SUPERPOWER.
THE OTHER JEWISH PROPHET IS LEFT TO PROPHESY TO THE HEATHEN ASSYRIANS.
...THE PROPHET DOOMS HIS OWN PEOPLE TO DESTRUCTION.
THAT PROPHET'S NAME IS YONA.

THE LORD APPOINTS TWO JEWISH PROPHETS TO PROPHESY TO YISRAEL AND ASHUR.
AMOS PROPHESIES TO HIS COMPATRIOTS.
HE FAILS.
THE MISSION IS AGONIZING, FOR IN SUCCESS...

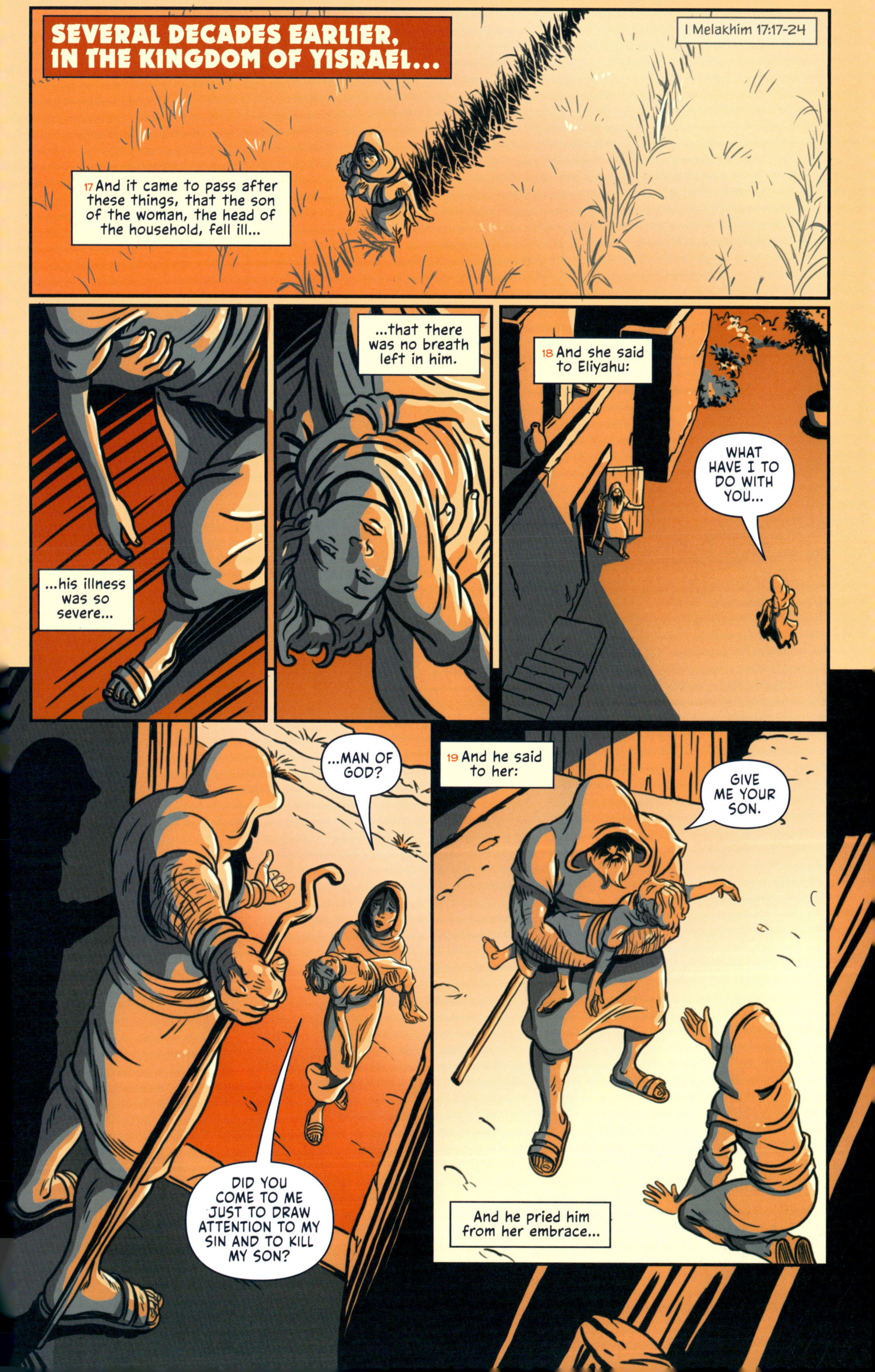
SEVERAL DECADES EARLIER, IN THE KINGDOM OF YISRAEL...
I Melakhim 17:17-24
17 And it came to pass after these things, that the son of the woman, the head of the household, fell ill...
...his illness was so severe...
...that there was no breath left in him.
18 And she said to Eliyahu:
WHAT HAVE I TO DO WITH YOU...
...MAN OF GOD?
DID YOU COME TO ME JUST TO DRAW ATTENTION TO MY SIN AND TO KILL MY SON?
19 And he said to her:
GIVE ME YOUR SON.
And he pried him from her embrace...

מלכים א׳
יז:יז–כד

יז וַיְהִ֗י אַחַר֙ הַדְּבָרִ֣ים הָאֵ֔לֶּה
חָלָ֕ה בֶּן־הָאִשָּׁ֖ה בַּעֲלַ֣ת הַבָּ֑יִת
וַיְהִ֤י חָלְיוֹ֙ חָזָ֣ק מְאֹ֔ד
עַ֛ד אֲשֶׁ֥ר לֹא־נֽוֹתְרָה־בּ֖וֹ נְשָׁמָֽה׃
יח וַתֹּ֙אמֶר֙ אֶל־אֵ֣לִיָּ֔הוּ
מַה־לִּ֥י וָלָ֖ךְ אִ֣ישׁ הָאֱלֹהִ֑ים
בָּ֧אתָ אֵלַ֛י לְהַזְכִּ֥יר אֶת־עֲוֺנִ֖י
וּלְהָמִ֥ית אֶת־בְּנִֽי׃
יט וַיֹּ֥אמֶר אֵלֶ֖יהָ
תְּנִֽי־לִ֣י אֶת־בְּנֵ֑ךְ
וַיִּקָּחֵ֣הוּ מֵחֵיקָ֗הּ

* על פי פרקי דרבי אליעזר לג

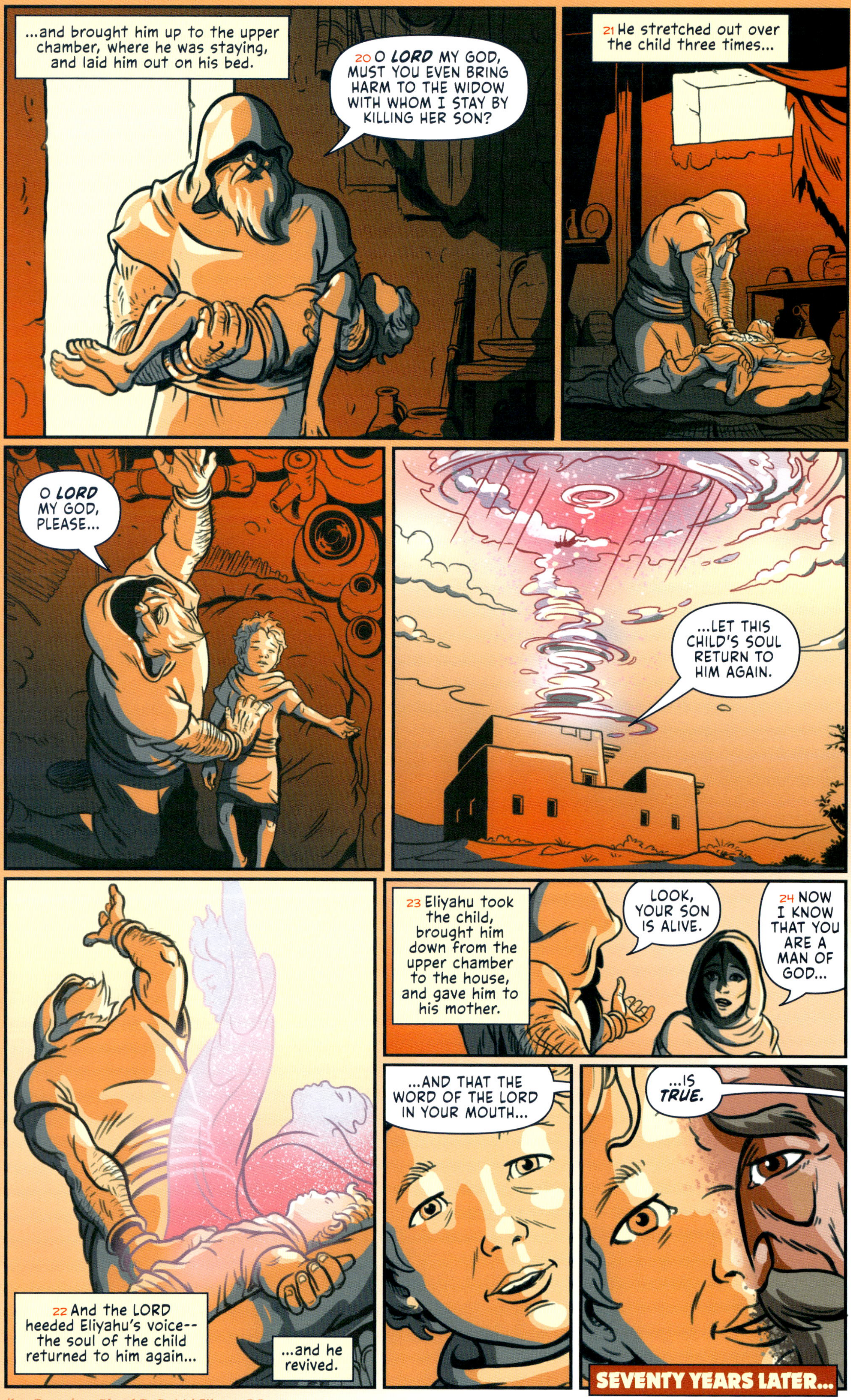
...and brought him up to the upper chamber, where he was staying, and laid him out on his bed.
20 O LORD MY GOD, MUST YOU EVEN BRING HARM TO THE WIDOW WITH WHOM I STAY BY KILLING HER SON?
21 He stretched out over the child three times...
O LORD MY GOD, PLEASE...
...LET THIS CHILD'S SOUL RETURN TO HIM AGAIN.
22 And the LORD heeded Eliyahu's voice--the soul of the child returned to him again...
...and he revived.
23 Eliyahu took the child, brought him down from the upper chamber to the house, and gave him to his mother.
LOOK, YOUR SON IS ALIVE.
24 NOW I KNOW THAT YOU ARE A MAN OF GOD...
...AND THAT THE WORD OF THE LORD IN YOUR MOUTH...
...IS TRUE.
SEVENTY YEARS LATER...

וַיַּעֲלֵ֨הוּ אֶל־הָעֲלִיָּ֜ה אֲשֶׁר־ה֣וּא יֹשֵׁ֥ב שָׁ֗ם
וַיַּשְׁכִּבֵ֖הוּ עַל־מִטָּתֽוֹ׃
כ וַיִּקְרָ֥א אֶל־יְהוָ֖ה וַיֹּאמַ֑ר
יְהוָ֣ה אֱלֹהָ֔י
הֲ֠גַם עַל־הָאַלְמָנָ֞ה
אֲשֶׁר־אֲנִ֨י מִתְגּוֹרֵ֥ר עִמָּ֛הּ
הֲרֵע֖וֹתָ לְהָמִ֥ית אֶת־בְּנָֽהּ׃
כא וַיִּתְמֹדֵ֤ד עַל־הַיֶּ֨לֶד֙ שָׁלֹ֣שׁ פְּעָמִ֔ים
וַיִּקְרָ֥א אֶל־יְהוָ֖ה וַיֹּאמַ֑ר
יְהוָ֣ה אֱלֹהָ֔י
תָּ֥שָׁב נָ֛א נֶֽפֶשׁ־הַיֶּ֥לֶד הַזֶּ֖ה עַל־קִרְבּֽוֹ׃
כב וַיִּשְׁמַ֥ע יְהוָ֖ה בְּק֣וֹל אֵלִיָּ֑הוּ
וַתָּ֧שָׁב נֶֽפֶשׁ־הַיֶּ֛לֶד עַל־קִרְבּ֖וֹ וַיֶּֽחִי׃
כג וַיִּקַּ֨ח אֵלִיָּ֜הוּ אֶת־הַיֶּ֗לֶד
וַיֹּרִדֵ֤הוּ מִן־הָעֲלִיָּה֙ הַבַּ֔יְתָה
וַֽיִּתְּנֵ֖הוּ לְאִמּ֑וֹ
וַיֹּ֨אמֶר֙ אֵלִיָּ֔הוּ רְאִ֖י חַ֥י בְּנֵֽךְ׃
כד וַתֹּ֤אמֶר הָֽאִשָּׁה֙ אֶל־אֵ֣לִיָּ֔הוּ
עַתָּה֙ זֶ֣ה יָדַ֔עְתִּי כִּ֛י אִ֥ישׁ אֱלֹהִ֖ים אָ֑תָּה
וּדְבַר־יְהוָ֥ה בְּפִ֖יךָ אֱמֶֽת׃

פרק א

CHAPTER 1

1 The word of the LORD came to Yona son of Amitai:
2 RISE UP
...GO TO THE GREAT CITY OF NINEVEH...
...AND CRY OUT AGAINST IT...

א וַֽיְהִי֙ דְּבַר־יְהוֹ֔ה
אֶל־יוֹנָ֥ה בֶן־אֲמִתַּ֖י
לֵאמֹֽר׃

ב ק֠וּם לֵ֧ךְ אֶל־נִֽינְוֵ֛ה
הָעִ֥יר הַגְּדוֹלָ֖ה
וּקְרָ֣א עָלֶ֑יהָ

...FOR ITS CRUEL EVIL HAS COME INTO MY SIGHT.
LIFE
DEATH
3 But Yona rose instead...
...to flee to Tarshish...
NINEVEH
נינוה
TARSHISH
תרשיש
...away from the LORD's presence.

כִּֽי־עָלְתָ֥ה
רָעָתָ֖ם
לְפָנָֽי׃

ג וַיָּ֤קָם יוֹנָה֙
לִבְרֹ֣חַ תַּרְשִׁ֔ישָׁה
מִלִּפְנֵ֖י יְהוָ֑ה

He went down to Yafo...
...found a ship bound for Tarshish...
...paid the fare...
...and went down inside the ship...
...to sail away with them to Tarshish...
...away from the LORD's presence.

וַיֵּ֣רֶד יָפ֗וֹ
וַיִּמְצָ֣א אָנִיָּ֣ה ׀ בָּאָ֣ה תַרְשִׁ֗ישׁ
וַיִּתֵּ֨ן שְׂכָרָ֜הּ
וַיֵּ֤רֶד בָּהּ֙
לָב֤וֹא עִמָּהֶם֙ תַּרְשִׁ֔ישָׁה
מִלִּפְנֵ֖י יְהוָֽה׃

4 But the LORD hurled a great wind across the sea.
A great storm overcame the sea...
...and the ship threatened to break apart.

ד וַֽיהוָ֗ה הֵטִ֤יל רֽוּחַ־גְּדוֹלָה֙ אֶל־הַיָּ֔ם
וַיְהִ֥י סַֽעַר־גָּד֖וֹל בַּיָּ֑ם
וְהָ֣אֳנִיָּ֔ה חִשְּׁבָ֖ה לְהִשָּׁבֵֽר׃

5 The sailors became frightened and cried out each to his god...
...and they cast the ship's cargo out into the sea to lighten the load...

ה וַיִּֽירְא֣וּ הַמַּלָּחִ֗ים
וַֽיִּזְעֲקוּ֮ אִ֣ישׁ אֶל־אֱלֹהָיו֒
וַיָּטִ֨לוּ אֶת־הַכֵּלִ֜ים אֲשֶׁ֤ר בָּאֳנִיָּה֙ אֶל־הַיָּ֔ם
לְהָקֵ֖ל מֵעֲלֵיהֶ֑ם

...But Yona went down to the bottom of the boat...
...lay down...
...and fell asleep.

וְיוֹנָ֗ה יָרַד֙ אֶל־יַרְכְּתֵ֣י הַסְּפִינָ֔ה
וַיִּשְׁכַּ֖ב וַיֵּרָדַֽם׃

6 The Captain came up to him.
HOW CAN YOU SLEEP?
RISE UP!
CRY OUT TO YOUR GOD!
PERHAPS YOUR GOD WILL THINK KINDLY OF US...
...AND WE...
...WILL NOT BE LOST.

ו וַיִּקְרַ֤ב אֵלָיו֙ רַ֣ב הַחֹבֵ֔ל
וַיֹּ֥אמֶר ל֖וֹ מַה־לְּךָ֣ נִרְדָּ֑ם
ק֚וּם קְרָ֣א אֶל־אֱלֹהֶ֔יךָ
אוּלַ֞י יִתְעַשֵּׁ֧ת הָאֱלֹהִ֛ים לָ֖נוּ
וְלֹ֥א נֹאבֵֽד׃

7 The sailors said to one another:
LET US CAST LOTS...
...SO THAT WE MAY KNOW ON WHOSE ACCOUNT THIS CRUEL EVIL HAS COME UPON US.
And they cast their lot...
...and the lot fell upon Yona.
8 They said to him:
TELL US--
--YOU FROM WHOM THIS CRUEL THING HAS COME--
WHAT IS YOUR TRADE AND WHERE ARE YOU COMING FROM?
WHICH COUNTRY IS YOURS, AND WHICH IS YOUR PEOPLE?

ז וַיֹּאמְרוּ אִישׁ אֶל־רֵעֵהוּ
לְכוּ וְנַפִּילָה גוֹרָלוֹת
וְנֵדְעָה בְּשֶׁלְּמִי הָרָעָה הַזֹּאת לָנוּ
וַיַּפִּלוּ גּוֹרָלוֹת
וַיִּפֹּל הַגּוֹרָל עַל־יוֹנָה:

ח וַיֹּאמְרוּ אֵלָיו
הַגִּידָה־נָּא לָנוּ
בַּאֲשֶׁר לְמִי־הָרָעָה הַזֹּאת לָנוּ
מַה־מְּלַאכְתְּךָ וּמֵאַיִן תָּבוֹא
מָה אַרְצֶךָ וְאֵי־מִזֶּה עַם אָתָּה:

9 And he said to them:
I AM A HEBREW--
...AND IT IS THE LORD GOD OF THE HEAVENS THAT I FEAR...
...HE WHO MADE BOTH SEA AND DRY LAND.

ט וַיֹּ֣אמֶר אֲלֵיהֶ֔ם
עִבְרִ֖י אָנֹ֑כִי
וְאֶת־יְהוָ֞ה אֱלֹהֵ֤י הַשָּׁמַ֙יִם֙ אֲנִ֣י יָרֵ֔א
אֲשֶׁר־עָשָׂ֥ה אֶת־הַיָּ֖ם וְאֶת־הַיַּבָּשָֽׁה׃

10 The men were filled with great fear and said:
WHAT HAVE YOU DONE?
--for they knew that he was fleeing the LORD's presence.
He had told them.
11 They said:
WHAT MUST WE DO TO YOU TO CALM THE SEA FOR US?
And the sea was storming ever more fiercely.

י וַיִּֽירְא֤וּ הָֽאֲנָשִׁים֙ יִרְאָ֣ה גְדוֹלָ֔ה
וַיֹּאמְר֥וּ אֵלָ֖יו
מַה־זֹּ֣את עָשִׂ֑יתָ
כִּֽי־יָדְע֣וּ הָֽאֲנָשִׁ֗ים
כִּֽי־מִלִּפְנֵ֤י יהוה֙ ה֣וּא בֹרֵ֔חַ
כִּ֥י הִגִּ֖יד לָהֶֽם׃

יא וַיֹּאמְר֤וּ אֵלָיו֙
מַה־נַּ֣עֲשֶׂה לָּ֔ךְ וְיִשְׁתֹּ֥ק הַיָּ֖ם מֵעָלֵ֑ינוּ
כִּ֥י הַיָּ֖ם הוֹלֵ֥ךְ וְסֹעֵֽר׃

12 He said:
LIFT ME UP--
CAST ME OUT INTO THE SEA...
...AND THE SEA WILL BE STILL FOR YOU...
...FOR I KNOW...
...THAT THIS...
...IT IS ON MY ACCOUNT...

יב וַיֹּאמֶר אֲלֵיהֶם
שָׂאוּנִי וַהֲטִילֻנִי אֶל־הַיָּם
וְיִשְׁתֹּק הַיָּם מֵעֲלֵיכֶם
כִּי יוֹדֵעַ אָנִי כִּי בְשֶׁלִּי

"...GREAT STORM..."

הַסַּעַר הַגָּדוֹל הַזֶּה

"...HAS COME UPON YOU."

עֲלֵיכֶם:

13 The men oared toward dry land...
...but could not reach it...
...for the sea was storming ever more fiercely around them.

יג וַיַּחְתְּר֣וּ הָֽאֲנָשִׁ֗ים
לְהָשִׁ֛יב אֶל־הַיַּבָּשָׁ֖ה
וְלֹ֣א יָכֹ֑לוּ
כִּ֣י הַיָּ֔ם הוֹלֵ֥ךְ וְסֹעֵ֖ר עֲלֵיהֶֽם׃

14 And they cried out to the LORD and said:
PLEASE, LORD...
...PLEASE--
...ON ACCOUNT OF THIS MAN'S LIFE...
...DO NOT LET US BE LOST...

יד וַיִּקְרְא֨וּ אֶל־יהו֜ה וַיֹּאמְר֗וּ

אָנָּ֤ה יהוה֙

אַל־נָ֣א נֹאבְדָ֗ה

בְּנֶ֙פֶשׁ֙ הָאִ֣ישׁ הַזֶּ֔ה

...AND DO NOT STAIN OUR HANDS...
...WITH INNOCENT BLOOD...
...FOR YOU ARE THE LORD--
...AND WHATEVER YOU DESIRE...
...YOU PERFORM.

וְאַל־תִּתֵּ֥ן עָלֵ֖ינוּ דָּ֣ם נָקִ֑יא
כִּֽי־אַתָּ֣ה יהו֔ה
כַּאֲשֶׁ֥ר חָפַ֖צְתָּ עָשִֽׂיתָ׃

15 And they lifted Yona up...
...and heaved him into the sea...
...and the sea stopped its raging.

טו וַיִּשְׂאוּ֙ אֶת־יוֹנָ֔ה
וַיְטִלֻ֖הוּ אֶל־הַיָּ֑ם
וַיַּעֲמֹ֥ד הַיָּ֖ם מִזַּעְפּֽוֹ׃

16 And the men were filled with a great fear of the LORD...
...and they offered up a sacrifice to the LORD...
...and made vows.

טז וַיִּֽירְא֧וּ הָאֲנָשִׁ֛ים יִרְאָ֥ה גְדוֹלָ֖ה אֶת־יְהוָ֑ה
וַיִּֽזְבְּחוּ־זֶ֙בַח֙ לַֽיהוָ֔ה
וַֽיִּדְּר֖וּ נְדָרִֽים׃

פרק ב

CHAPTER 2

1 The LORD...
...sent...
...a great fish...

א וַיְמַ֤ן יהוה֙
דָּ֣ג גָּד֔וֹל

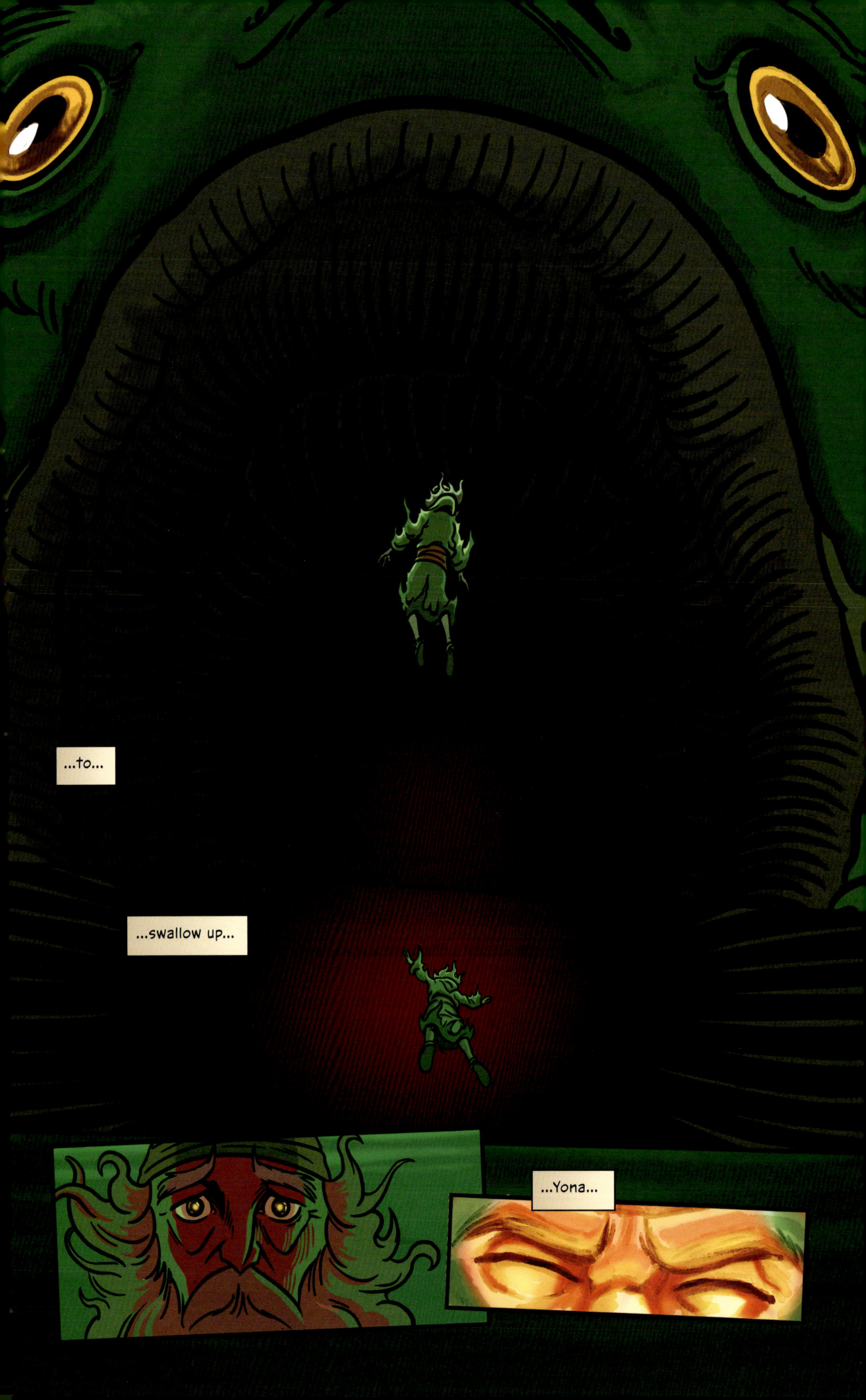
...to...
...swallow up...
...Yona...

לִבְלֹ֖עַ אֶת־יוֹנָ֑ה

...and Yona...
...was inside the belly of the fish for three days...

וַיְהִ֤י יוֹנָה֙
בִּמְעֵ֣י הַדָּ֔ג
שְׁלֹשָׁ֥ה יָמִ֖ים

...and three nights.

וּשְׁלֹשָׁה לֵילוֹת:

2 And Yona prayed to the LORD his God from the belly of the fish:
3 FROM A NARROW PLACE I CRY OUT TO THE LORD, AND HE WILL ANSWER.
FROM THE BELLY OF SHEOL, I BEG YOU--
...HEAR MY WORDS.

ב וַיִּתְפַּלֵּל יוֹנָה אֶל־יהוה אֱלֹהָיו
מִמְּעֵי הַדָּגָה׃

ג וַיֹּאמֶר
קָרָאתִי מִצָּרָה לִי אֶל־יהוה
וַיַּעֲנֵנִי
מִבֶּטֶן שְׁאוֹל שִׁוַּעְתִּי
שָׁמַעְתָּ קוֹלִי׃

4 YOU HAVE
CAST ME DOWN
INTO DEEP WATERS
THE HEART
OF THE SEA...

ד וַתַּשְׁלִיכֵ֤נִי מְצוּלָה֙ בִּלְבַ֣ב יַמִּ֔ים

...THE CURRENT ENGULFS ME...
...ALL YOUR TORRENTS AND STORM WAVES CRASH OVER ME.
5 I SAID TO MYSELF, I AM FLUNG AWAY OUT OF YOUR PRESENCE...
...BUT I WILL YET SEE YOUR HOLY SANCTUARY AGAIN.

וְנָהָ֖ר יְסֹבְבֵ֑נִי
כָּל־מִשְׁבָּרֶ֥יךָ וְגַלֶּ֖יךָ עָלַ֥י עָבָֽרוּ׃

ה וַאֲנִ֣י אָמַ֔רְתִּי
נִגְרַ֖שְׁתִּי מִנֶּ֣גֶד עֵינֶ֑יךָ
אַ֚ךְ אוֹסִ֣יף לְהַבִּ֔יט אֶל־הֵיכַ֖ל קָדְשֶֽׁךָ׃

6 THE WATERS RUSH AROUND ME TO MY VERY LIFE'S EDGE...
...DEEPS SURROUND ME...

ו אֲפָפ֤וּנִי מַ֙יִם֙ עַד־נֶ֔פֶשׁ
תְּה֖וֹם יְסֹבְבֵ֑נִי

...WEEDS CROWN ME.
7 I HAVE SUNK DOWN TO THE ROOTS OF THE HILLS...
...THE EARTH IS FOREVER BARRED BEFORE ME.
YET YOU RAISE MY LIFE UP FROM THE ABYSS, O LORD MY GOD.

סוּף חָבוּשׁ לְרֹאשִׁי׃

לְקִצְבֵי הָרִים יָרַדְתִּי ז
הָאָרֶץ בְּרִחֶיהָ בַעֲדִי לְעוֹלָם
וַתַּעַל מִשַּׁחַת חַיַּי
יְהוָה אֱלֹהָי׃

8 AS MY LIFE CLOSES OVER ME...
...THE *LORD* COMES TO MY MIND--
...THEN MY PRAYER COMES TO YOU...
...COMES TO YOUR HOLY SANCTUARY.
9 THOSE WHO CLEAVE TO EMPTY FOLLY...
...WILL YET FORSAKE THEIR FAITHFULNESS.

ח בְּהִתְעַטֵּ֤ף עָלַי֙ נַפְשִׁ֔י
אֶת־יהו֖ה זָכָ֑רְתִּי
וַתָּב֤וֹא אֵלֶ֙יךָ֙ תְּפִלָּתִ֔י
אֶל־הֵיכַ֖ל קָדְשֶֽׁךָ׃

ט מְשַׁמְּרִ֖ים הַבְלֵי־שָׁ֑וְא
חַסְדָּ֖ם יַעֲזֹֽבוּ׃

10 BUT I, VOICING THANKS...
...SHALL BRING YOU OFFERINGS.
I SHALL FULFILL...
...WHAT I HAVE VOWED.

י וַאֲנִ֗י בְּק֤וֹל תּוֹדָה֙
אֶזְבְּחָה־לָּ֔ךְ
אֲשֶׁ֥ר נָדַ֖רְתִּי אֲשַׁלֵּ֑מָה

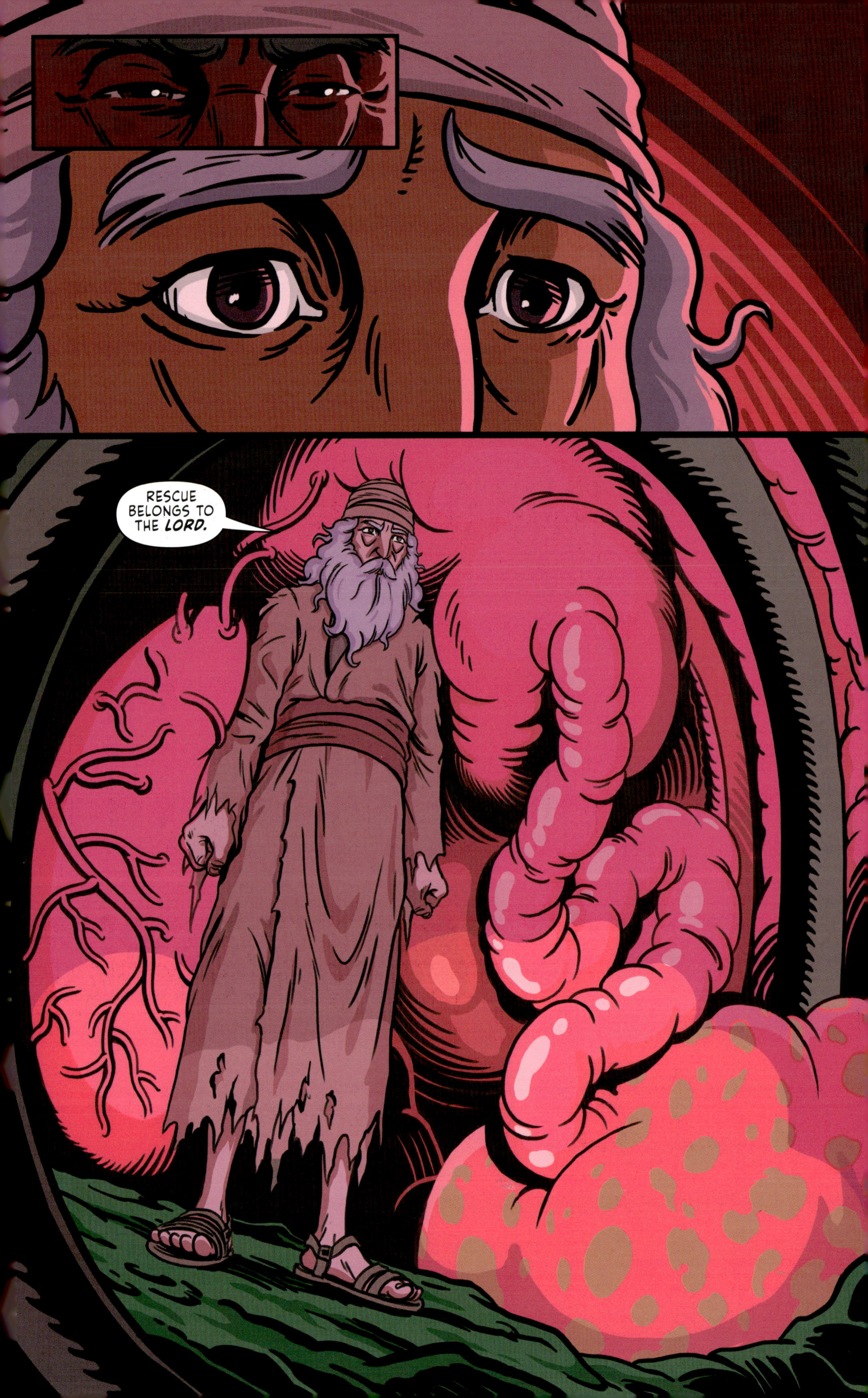
RESCUE BELONGS TO THE LORD.

יְשׁוּעָתָה לַיהוָה:

יא וַיֹּ֥אמֶר יְהֹוָ֖ה לַדָּ֑ג
וַיָּ֥קֵא אֶת־יוֹנָ֖ה אֶל־הַיַּבָּשָֽׁה׃

11 And the LORD spoke to the fish...
...and it vomited Yona out...

פרק ג

CHAPTER 3

1 So the word of the LORD came to Yona for a second time:

2 RISE UP--
GO TO THE GREAT CITY OF NINEVEH AND CRY OUT TO IT THE CALL THAT I CONVEY TO YOU.

א **וַ֠יְהִ֧י** דְבַר־יְהוָ֛ה אֶל־יוֹנָ֖ה שֵׁנִ֥ית לֵאמֹֽר׃

ב ק֛וּם לֵ֥ךְ אֶל־נִֽינְוֵ֖ה הָעִ֣יר הַגְּדוֹלָ֑ה
וּקְרָ֤א אֵלֶ֙יהָ֙ אֶת־הַקְּרִיאָ֔ה
אֲשֶׁ֥ר אָנֹכִ֖י דֹּבֵ֥ר אֵלֶֽיךָ׃

3 And Yona rose...
NINEVEH
נינוה
TARSHISH
תרשיש
NINEVEH
נינוה
TARSHISH
תרשיש

ג וַיָּ֣קָם יוֹנָ֗ה

...and went to Nineveh
as the LORD had said.

וַיֵּלֶךְ אֶל־נִינְוֵה
כִּדְבַר יְהֹוָה

Nineveh was an immensely great city, three days' walk across.
4 Yona began his journey, a day's walk into Nineveh...
...and cried out:

וְנִֽינְוֵ֗ה הָיְתָ֤ה עִיר־גְּדוֹלָה֙ לֵֽאלֹהִ֔ים
מַהֲלַ֖ךְ שְׁלֹ֥שֶׁת יָמִֽים׃

ד וַיָּ֤חֶל יוֹנָה֙ לָב֣וֹא בָעִ֔יר
מַהֲלַ֖ךְ י֣וֹם אֶחָ֑ד
וַיִּקְרָא֙ וַיֹּאמַ֔ר

FORTY MORE DAYS...
40
...AND NINEVEH WILL BE OVERTURNED!

ע֗וֹד אַרְבָּעִ֣ים י֔וֹם
וְנִֽינְוֵ֖ה נֶהְפָּֽכֶת׃

5 And the people of Nineveh...
...believed in God...
...and declared a fast...
...and dressed themselves in sackcloth...
...from the greatest of them...
...to the least.

ה וַיַּאֲמִ֛ינוּ אַנְשֵׁ֥י נִֽינְוֵ֖ה בֵּֽאלֹהִ֑ים
וַיִּקְרְאוּ־צוֹם֙
וַיִּלְבְּשׁ֣וּ שַׂקִּ֔ים
מִגְּדוֹלָ֖ם וְעַד־קְטַנָּֽם׃

6 When word reached...
...the king of Nineveh...
40
...he rose from his throne...
...took off his mantle...
...covered himself with sackcloth...
...and sat down upon ashes.

ו וַיִּגַּ֤ע הַדָּבָר֙ אֶל־מֶ֣לֶךְ נִֽינְוֵ֔ה
וַיָּ֙קָם֙ מִכִּסְא֔וֹ
וַיַּעֲבֵ֥ר אַדַּרְתּ֖וֹ מֵעָלָ֑יו
וַיְכַ֣ס שַׂ֔ק
וַיֵּ֖שֶׁב עַל־הָאֵֽפֶר׃

7 And he had this proclaimed in Nineveh in the name of the king and his nobles:
"NO PERSON OR ANIMAL-- CATTLE OR FLOCK-- MAY TASTE ANY MORSEL...
"THEY MAY NOT PASTURE...
"THEY MAY DRINK NO WATER."
8 "ALL MUST BE COVERED IN SACKCLOTH, MAN AND BEAST, AND MUST CRY OUT TO GOD WITH ALL THEIR STRENGTH...
"LET EVERY MAN TURN BACK FROM HIS CRUEL PRACTICES, FROM THE VIOLENCE THAT STAINS HIS HANDS."
9 WHO KNOWS? PERHAPS GOD, TOO, WILL TURN BACK AND RELENT, WILL TURN BACK FROM HIS BURNING RAGE BEFORE WE ARE ALL LOST.

ז וַיַּזְעֵ֗ק וַיֹּ֙אמֶר֙ בְּנִֽינְוֵ֔ה
מִטַּ֧עַם הַמֶּ֛לֶךְ וּגְדֹלָ֖יו לֵאמֹ֑ר
הָאָדָ֨ם וְהַבְּהֵמָ֜ה הַבָּקָ֣ר וְהַצֹּ֗אן
אַֽל־יִטְעֲמוּ֙ מְא֔וּמָה
אַל־יִרְע֔וּ
וּמַ֖יִם אַל־יִשְׁתּֽוּ׃

ח וְיִתְכַּסּ֣וּ שַׂקִּ֗ים הָֽאָדָם֙ וְהַבְּהֵמָ֔ה
וְיִקְרְא֥וּ אֶל־אֱלֹהִ֖ים בְּחָזְקָ֑ה
וְיָשֻׁ֗בוּ אִ֚ישׁ מִדַּרְכּ֣וֹ הָֽרָעָ֔ה
וּמִן־הֶחָמָ֖ס אֲשֶׁ֥ר בְּכַפֵּיהֶֽם׃

ט מִֽי־יוֹדֵ֣עַ יָשׁ֔וּב וְנִחַ֖ם הָאֱלֹהִ֑ים
וְשָׁ֛ב מֵחֲר֥וֹן אַפּ֖וֹ וְלֹ֥א נֹאבֵֽד׃

10 ...AND GOD SAW THEIR ACTIONS...
...that they had turned away from their cruel practices.

י וַיַּרְא הָאֱלֹהִים אֶת־מַעֲשֵׂיהֶם
כִּי־שָׁבוּ מִדַּרְכָּם הָרָעָה

...And God relented from the evil He had spoken of bringing upon them...

...and brought it not.

וַיִּנָּ֣חֶם הָאֱלֹהִ֔ים עַל־הָרָעָ֛ה
אֲשֶׁר־דִּבֶּ֥ר לַעֲשׂוֹת־לָהֶ֖ם
וְלֹ֥א עָשָֽׂה׃

פרק ד

CHAPTER 4

1 To Yona this was a cruel evil...
...and he raged against it.
YISRAEL
2 And he prayed to the LORD and said...
PLEASE, ***LORD,*** IS THIS NOT JUST WHAT I SAID WHILE I WAS STILL IN MY OWN LAND?
THIS IS WHY I FIRST FLED TOWARD TARSHISH...

א **וַיֵּ֥רַע** אֶל־יוֹנָ֖ה רָעָ֣ה גְדוֹלָ֑ה
וַיִּ֖חַר לֽוֹ׃

ב וַיִּתְפַּלֵּ֨ל אֶל־יהו֜ה וַיֹּאמַ֗ר
אָנָּ֤ה יהוה֙
הֲלוֹא־זֶ֣ה דְבָרִ֔י
עַד־הֱיוֹתִי֙ עַל־אַדְמָתִ֔י
עַל־כֵּ֥ן קִדַּ֖מְתִּי לִבְרֹ֣חַ תַּרְשִׁ֑ישָׁה

...BECAUSE I KNEW THAT YOU ARE A GRACIOUS AND COMPASSIONATE GOD...
יונה
בן
אמתי
...SLOW TO ANGER...
אמת
...ABOUNDING IN KINDNESS...
אמת
...AND RELENTING FROM EVIL.

כִּ֣י יָדַ֗עְתִּי
כִּ֤י אַתָּה֙ אֵֽל־חַנּ֣וּן וְרַח֔וּם
אֶ֤רֶךְ אַפַּ֙יִם֙
וְרַב־חֶ֔סֶד
וְנִחָ֖ם עַל־הָרָעָֽה׃

3 NOW, LORD, PLEASE TAKE MY SOUL AWAY FROM ME, FOR DEATH WOULD BE BETTER THAN MY LIFE.
4 ARE YOU SO ENRAGED?
...said the LORD.

ג וְעַתָּ֣ה יהו֔ה
קַח־נָ֥א אֶת־נַפְשִׁ֖י מִמֶּ֑נִּי
כִּ֛י ט֥וֹב מוֹתִ֖י מֵחַיָּֽי׃

ד וַיֹּ֣אמֶר יהו֔ה
הַהֵיטֵ֖ב חָ֥רָה לָֽךְ׃

5 Yona left the city...
...and sat down to its east...
He made himself a shelter...
...and sat in the shade beneath it...
...waiting to see...
...what would become...
...of the city.

ה וַיֵּצֵ֤א יוֹנָה֙ מִן־הָעִ֔יר
וַיֵּ֖שֶׁב מִקֶּ֣דֶם לָעִ֑יר
וַיַּעַשׂ֩ ל֨וֹ שָׁ֜ם סֻכָּ֗ה
וַיֵּ֤שֶׁב תַּחְתֶּ֙יהָ֙ בַּצֵּ֔ל
עַ֚ד אֲשֶׁ֣ר יִרְאֶ֔ה מַה־יִּהְיֶ֖ה בָּעִֽיר׃

6 The LORD God sent a gourd plant...
...which grew up above Yona to shade his head...
...to shield him from the cruel heat...
...and Yona rejoiced over this gourd plant with great joy.

ו וַיְמַ֣ן יְהוָֽה־אֱ֠לֹהִ֠ים קִ֞יקָי֗וֹן
וַיַּ֣עַל ׀ מֵעַ֣ל לְיוֹנָ֗ה
לִהְי֥וֹת צֵל֙ עַל־רֹאשׁ֔וֹ
לְהַצִּ֥יל ל֖וֹ מֵרָעָת֑וֹ
וַיִּשְׂמַ֥ח יוֹנָ֛ה עַל־הַקִּיקָי֖וֹן
שִׂמְחָ֥ה גְדוֹלָֽה׃

7 But God sent...
...a worm as dawn broke the next day...
...and it attacked...
...the gourd plant...
...until it dried up entirely.

ז וַיְמַ֤ן הָֽאֱלֹהִים֙ תּוֹלַ֔עַת
בַּעֲל֥וֹת הַשַּׁ֖חַר לַֽמָּחֳרָ֑ת
וַתַּ֥ךְ אֶת־הַקִּֽיקָי֖וֹן וַיִּיבָֽשׁ׃

8 As the sun rose...
...God...
...sent a scorching east wind...
...and the sun beat down on Yona's head.

ח וַיְהִ֣י ׀ כִּזְרֹ֣חַ הַשֶּׁ֗מֶשׁ
וַיְמַ֨ן אֱלֹהִ֜ים ר֤וּחַ קָדִים֙ חֲרִישִׁ֔ית
וַתַּ֥ךְ הַשֶּׁ֛מֶשׁ עַל־רֹ֥אשׁ יוֹנָ֖ה

He grew faint and asked that he might die.
DEATH...
...WOULD BE BETTER...
...THAN MY LIFE.
9 God said to Yona:
ARE YOU SO ENRAGED ABOUT THE GOURD PLANT?
I AM ENRAGED ENOUGH TO DIE.
10 YOU CARED ABOUT THAT GOURD PLANT...
...WHICH YOU DID NOT TOIL FOR AND DID NOT GROW...
...WHICH WAS BORN OVERNIGHT...
...AND WAS LOST OVERNIGHT.

וַיִּתְעַלָּף וַיִּשְׁאַל אֶת־נַפְשׁוֹ לָמוּת
וַיֹּאמֶר טוֹב מוֹתִי מֵחַיָּי׃

ט וַיֹּאמֶר אֱלֹהִים אֶל־יוֹנָה
הַהֵיטֵב חָרָה־לְךָ עַל־הַקִּיקָיוֹן
וַיֹּאמֶר הֵיטֵב חָרָה־לִי עַד־מָוֶת׃

י וַיֹּאמֶר יהוה
אַתָּה חַסְתָּ עַל־הַקִּיקָיוֹן
אֲשֶׁר לֹא־עָמַלְתָּ בּוֹ וְלֹא גִדַּלְתּוֹ
שֶׁבִּן־לַיְלָה הָיָה
וּבִן־לַיְלָה אָבָד׃

11 AM I NOT TO CARE FOR THE GREAT CITY OF NINEVEH...
...WHICH HAS IN IT MORE THAN ONE HUNDRED AND TWENTY THOUSAND PEOPLE...
...WHO DO NOT KNOW THEIR RIGHT HANDS FROM THEIR LEFT, AND SO MANY ANIMALS?

יא וַאֲנִי֙ לֹ֣א אָח֔וּס
עַל־נִֽינְוֵ֖ה הָעִ֣יר הַגְּדוֹלָ֑ה
אֲשֶׁ֣ר יֶשׁ־בָּ֡הּ
הַרְבֵּה֩ מִֽשְׁתֵּים־עֶשְׂרֵ֨ה רִבּ֜וֹ אָדָ֗ם
אֲשֶׁ֤ר לֹֽא־יָדַע֙ בֵּין־יְמִינ֣וֹ לִשְׂמֹאל֔וֹ
וּבְהֵמָ֖ה רַבָּֽה׃

BIBLIOGRAPHY

Tanakh

I Melakhim 6, 12, 17, 20, 21
II Melakhim 10, 13, 14
Hoshea 5
Yoel 2
Amos 1, 2, 6, 7, 8
Mikha 7
Naḥum 1-3
II Divrei Hayamim 26

Classic Commentaries on Yona

Abrabanel
Ibn Ezra
Malbim
Metzudat David
Metzudat Tzion
Perush HaGra
Radak
Rashi

Ḥazal

Mekhilta DeRabbi Shimon ben Yochai
Mekhilta DeRabbi Yishmael
Midrash Tanḥuma
Midrash Tehillim
Midrash Rabba
Midrash Yona
Pirkei DeRabbi Eliezer
Sefer HaZohar
Yalkut Shimoni – Yona

Mishna

Tractate Taanit 2:1,4

Tosefta

Tractate Sanhedrin 14:4

Talmud

Y. Tractate Berakhot 9:1
Y. Tractate Eiruvin 10:1
Y. Tractate Sukka 1:2, 5:1
Y. Tractate Taanit 2:1
Y. Tractate Sanhedrin 11:5
Tractate Eiruvin 96a
Tractate Taanit 16a
Tractate Yevamot 98a
Tractate Nedarim 38a, 51b
Tractate Gittin 31b
Tractate Sanhedrin 89a, 89b

Contemporary Commentaries on Yona (Hebrew)

Ben-Menahem, Elyakim. *Trei Asar*. Mosad Harav Kook, 1990.

Simon, Uriel. "*Yona*." In *Mikra LeYisrael: Perush Mada'i LaMikra – Ovadia-Yona*. Magnes Press, 1992.

Steinsaltz, Rabbi Adin Even-Israel. *HaTanakh HaMevo'ar: Sefer Trei-Asar*. Koren Publishers, 2016.

Zakovitch, Yair and Avigdor Shinan. *Sefer Yona: Perush Yisraeli Ḥadash*. Yedioth Books, 2015.

Zakovitch, Yair. "*Sefer Yona*." In *Olam HaTanakh: Trei Asar I*, edited by Prof. Ze'ev Weisman. Divrei Hayamim, 2002.

Contemporary Books (Hebrew)

Lau, Rabbi Binyamin. *Shemona Nevi'im: BaAvotot Ahava.* Yedioth Books, 2016.

Lichtenstein, Rabbi Moshe. *Netivei Nevua: Mabat el HaHaftarot.* Maggid Books, 2015.

Medan, Rabbi Yaakov. *HaMikraot HaMitḥadshim: Iyunim BiNvi'im UviKhtuvim.* Herzog College Press – Tevunot, 2015.

Rivlin, Rabbi Avraham. *Yona: Nevua VeTokheḥa.* Yeshivat Kerem B'Yavne, 1999.

Yeshivat Har Etzion. *Be'er Miriam: Yom HaKipurim.* Yedioth Books, 2013.

Koren Tanakh LeMetayel. Koren Publishers, 2022.

Contemporary Books (English)

The Koren Sacks Yom Kippur Maḥzor. Koren Publishers, 2016.

Brown, Dr. Erica. *Jonah: The Reluctant Prophet.* Maggid Books, 2017.

Jachter, Rabbi Chaim and Binyamin Jachter. *Depths of Yonah: Unleashing the Power of Your Yom Kippur.* 2023.

Klitsner, Judy. *Subversive Sequels in the Bible: How Biblical Stories Mine and Undermine Each Other.* Maggid Books, 2019.

Wein, Rabbi Berel. *Who Knows Twelve? Themes and Values in Trei Asar.* Maggid Books, 2015.

Online Resources

929.org

AlHatorah.org

Hatanakh.com

The Israel Koschitzky Torat Har Etzion VBM, https://etzion.org.il/en

- Freedman, Rabbi Binny. "*Sefer Yonah* – Does It Matter?" 2018.
- Grossman, Prof. Yonatan. "*Keria Sifrutit BeSefer Yona.*" 2018. [Hebrew]
- Jotkowitz, Prof. Alan. "Reading Yona with the Rambam, the Rav, and R. Lichtenstein." 2019.
- Klein, Dr. Neriah. "*Yona.*" 2015. [Hebrew]
- Lichtenstein, Rabbi Mosheh. "Yona: Everyman's *Teshuva.*" 2015.
- Medan, Rabbi Yaakov. "*Yona Le'umat Arba'a Nevi'im.*" 2019. [Hebrew]
- Taragin, Rabbanit Shani. "Yonah." 2012.

Ori Levi
Rachel Max
Additional Color

Shira Avigad
Additional Layouts

Sarah Quintas
Research Assistant

Zachary Joseph
Editorial Assistant

Andrew Galitzer
Summer Intern Manager

Summer Interns

Koby Desmond
Dovi "Daredevil" Deutsch
Josh Diamont
Yona Kelman
Josh Weichbrod

Advisors

Rabbi Mitch Berkowitz
Rabbi Avi Billet
Kate Davis
Nili Isenberg
Jesse Orenshein
Rabbi David Vaisberg

To my holy wife and children. I'm so glad Hashem chose us for each other. May it be for long years filled with health, happiness, and joy.
—David

In loving memory of
Yaron Eliezer Chitiz *z"l,*
and each of the courageous soldiers and civilians who have made the ultimate sacrifice in our defense.
—The JewishCartoon.com Team

Appreciation

Amy, Ashira, Eliana, Noam & Ori Gorfinkel • Binyomin, Tzvi, Esther, Chaim, Meir, Shira & Shlomo Ginzberg • Yafit, Reiut, Matan, Adeev & Hadar Cohn • Shahar Tamir Nathan • Erez, Lena, May & Aviv Zadok • Jennifer & Grant Dinner • Shawni Modrell-Astrof & Jeff Astrof • Dr. Yael & Jeffrey Halaas • Rachel & Alex Katz & Family • Rebecca & David Kekst & Family • Daphne & Jonathan Orenshein • Allyson Gronowitz • Robin & Josh Rochlin • Ronnie Buchman & Andrew Schonzeit • Hindy & Ruby Taub • Dana & Joel Gorfinkel • Batsheva & Sheldon Kasdan • Debi Pomerantz & Michael Mendelson • Ceil & David Olivestone • Debbie & Avner Parnes • Rachel, Mark, Samantha, Aaron & Zachary Hecht • Tamir Hason • Scott Peterson • Mark Chiarello • Tova & Gerald Segal & Family • Lisa Klink • Dave Matkowsky • Aaron Sowd • Fabrice Sapolsky • Rabbi Jason & Lauren Weiner & Family • Rich Rabinovich • Israel Animation College • NSN: The Nachum Segal Network • NJ Jewish Link • Atlanta Jewish Times • American Jewish World • The Good Guys & the Class of '85 • The countless communities around the world who have hosted @JewishCartoon presentations & programming

Hakarat Hatov to the Gorfinkel, Ginzberg & Chitiz spouses and children for their support throughout all the long days and all-nighters.

At Koren, heartfelt *hakarat hatov* to Matthew Miller, Yehoshua Miller, Daniel Rose, Avishai Magence, Reuven Ziegler, Ita Olesker, Efrat Gross, Avichai Gamdani, Caryn Meltz, Tani Bayer, Aryeh Grossman, Alex Drucker, Doron Chitiz, Rina Ben Gal, Shlomo Peterseil, Shari Fisch, Gabi Rosenthal, and the incomparable Gila Chitiz.

Sincere apologies to anyone whom we inadvertently overlooked; we welcome corrections for future editions.

Jordan B. Gorfinkel "Gorf"
Creator, Producer & Editor

David Sacks
Writer

Rob Leigh
Letterer

Tzipora Ginzberg
Managing Editor
Production & Design

Dr. Moshe Cohn
Editor At Large

Darren J. Vincenzo
Talent Manager

Eliana Gorfinkel
Administrative Associate

Tzvi Ginzberg
Assistant Editor

Larisa Kerzhner
Dave Youkovich
Artists: Chapters 1, 3, and 4

Avi Blyer
Artist: Cover; Prologues 1 and 3; Chapter 2

Aaron Minier
Artist: Prologue 2
Storytelling Layouts: Chapters 1-4
Cover Layout

Yael Nathan
Color: Cover; Prologue 1; Chapter 1 (pages 2-6); Chapters 3-4

Shani Grim
Color: Chapter 1 (pages 8-36)
Dedication Page Illustration

Dannel Reskala
Color: Prologues 2-3; Chapter 2 (pages 64-65)

Yvel Guichet
Storytelling Layouts: Prologue 3

KOREN

Rabbi Avishai Magence
Editor-in-Chief

Gila Chitiz
Project Manager

Jessica Sacks
Translator

Rina Ben Gal
Hebrew Typesetting

Rabbi Doron Chitiz
Research Scholar

Ita Olesker
Efrat Gross
Avichai Gamdani
Proofreaders

Behind the Scenes artwork:
Larisa Kerzhner and Avi Blyer

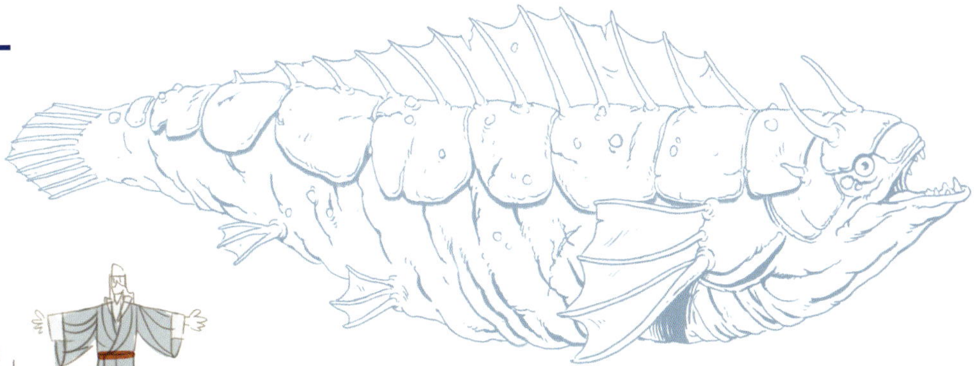

The King of Nineveh

JEWISH CARTOON .com

KORKEN